Then & Now
CHORLEY

At a three1way junction formed by Market Street, Bolton Street and Pall Mall stood the National School from 1825. This later became St George's School, with adjoining institute. The men of the institute appear to have enjoyed building celebratory archways of wood for special occasions. Here, at the end of Pall Mall looking into Market Street, an archway has been built to celebrate the forthcoming Coronation of King Edward VII in June 1902. Another feature of interest here is a large cast iron lamp post, referred to as the 'big lamp', just visible to the right.

Then & Now
CHORLEY

COMPILED BY J. SMITH

First published 2001

Tempus Publishing Limited
The Mill, Brimscombe Port,
Stroud, Gloucestershire, GL5 2QG

ISBN 0 7524 2278 2

Typesetting and origination by
Tempus Publishing Limited
Printed in Great Britain by
Midway Colour Print, Wiltshire

The church 'Walk of Witness' is still an annual event in Chorley, when, in the year 2000, the three denominational churches walked together for the first time. In this 1920s photograph, taken in the town's Market Street, the church banner with its attendants from the Roman Catholic church of Weldbank passes the watching crowds.

The coming of the motor coach proved to be very popular, and was a welcome improvement on the open sided charabanc, due to the added warmth and dryness for the passengers. In Chorley, the coach firm of Messrs Parsons led the way in trips to the seaside during the 1920s. In this view, the coach is stopped for refreshments at the Roe Buck Inn, a few miles north of Chorley, in the village of Whittle le Woods.

Contents

The town's first baths were built during 1906-07, by the Men's Guild of St Mary's Roman Catholic church, close to the church itself. In the photograph, excavation work for the open-air pool is well underway. In 1929, the pool was made available to local schools. The pool was closed the same year as new public baths were opened in Chorley, in 1938.

Acknowledgements

The author would like to thank the following for their help and advice in the compilation of this book.

Friends and colleagues of the Chorley and District Historical and Archaeological society; Chorley Central Library and other local branch libraries; the *Chorley Guardian* newspaper, for permission to use photographs as purchased years ago by their readers, which appear in the book; and the *Chorley Citizen* newspaper. Thanks also to Gregg Culshaw and Brian Straw, newsagents; Spar and Co-op shops, and several other Chorley shops, for allowing me to advertise for material; Messrs Turner and Co. (Photographers), Leyland, for processing work; Barrie and Teresa Holding; Bob and Pat Catterall; John and Evelyn Smith; and any other contributors to the book whom I have not previously mentioned.

A special thank you to Cath Halstead, sometime mentor and advisor, who gave encouragement and support at times when the way forward was unclear.

INTRODUCTION

The title of this book at first suggests rather a straightforward way to compile a number of photographs, illustrating what a particular place (in this instance, the town of Chorley in Lancashire) looked like years ago – then – compared with the present day – now. However, one of the problems with such a book is that the older 'then' photographs can only date from the middle of the nineteenth century at the earliest. Even then, if photographs do exist, it is likely that they will be family portraits or groups.

Any other subjects selected by the photographers of the mid-nineteenth century were rather limited in their scope, favouring scenes such as buildings due to their non-movement. By the 1880s, the work of the photographer was expanding, and a greater range of subjects was possible, including people and activities. Some of these are interesting, in that they show groups of people all supposed to be standing perfectly still for a long time, but this was not the case in many photographs, where images of people are blurred, due to a person moving as the shutter was pressed.

Of the photographs I have been able to amass in my own collection of old images of Chorley and its districts, the oldest date from the 1860s, one of which I will be using in the subsequent pages. Some of the images have been obtained from glass negatives, which, surprisingly, were in use until the early 1960s. Thus any old images of the town can only date from that time, and will be limited in their subject matter; they cannot reflect what the town looked like before that date. For that information we must refer to descriptions in old directories and newspapers, but even then illustrations were not used. However, from the descriptions we are able to get a good idea what the buildings of the town looked like.

No doubt many of the old photographic images of Chorley have been lost or thrown away, perhaps due to being unwanted by a family, or maybe destroyed as the property of businesses which have since come to an end. Yet if they were donated to local libraries instead, many more images of the past would remain, as a part of our present!

In Chorley, the town itself developed from each side of the main street, between the present Pall Mall and the parish church of St Laurence, with small outlying independent communities at Pall Mall, Moor Road, Bolton Street and Botany. These communities gradually joined up, mills were built, along with more houses, shops, schools and so on. The Lancaster Canal was built through the town in 1797, and the railway from 1841 to 1843. Sadly, no photographic images survive to show us how this work was done, yet we know from documentary sources that the job needed a large workforce.

Due to my deep involvement with local history, researching the past has meant that I have become aware of how much the town has changed from the past (then), to the present (now), from the mid-nineteenth century right up until the twenty-first century. The selection of photographic images which follows will ensure that more people in the town will realise just how much the town has changed, by comparing old images and new.

Perhaps the greatest change that has come about within the town of Chorley during our chosen historical period has been the removal of old property and its replacement by many council estates. Much of this old property was built in the early nineteenth century, for the purpose of handloom weaving in the cellars. These terraced cottages could be entered by steps to the front door, and were equipped with windows at pavement level, in order to allow light into the cellars where the looms were situated.

Much of this very old property was still in use into the 1950s, when it was finally condemned, but many residents still did not want to leave their old homes, despite their poor condition. So too, with the numerous large cotton mills of the town. At one time, over twenty of these, all with their tall chimneys, dominated the skyline. Today there is one survivor, which has a preservation order on it, partly through my intervention. Of the mills themselves, only one remains in use, and those others still standing have now found a new lease of life, as multiple units and bowling or snooker clubs.

On the social side of life in Chorley, the dancehall and cinema predominated until their decline in the 1950s and '60s. Today the cinema in Chorley is non-existent, and the dancehall survives only as a multi-purpose function room, used for various events. The town centre has seen many changes over the past few years, such as the introduction of a shopping mall and the pedestrianization of some streets. The local hospital has been enlarged greatly, while two other older local hospitals have been demolished.

Within the following pages, I can only illustrate a few of those changes with photographs of Chorley, but I hope these will evoke a few memories, and stimulate some conversations.

Jack Smith
Chorley, May 2001

Chapter 1
Street Scenes

The street passing between the two markets in Chorley is called New Market Street, here seen looking towards Chapel Street in the distance. This view certainly dates from before 1914, for that year the all-wood theatre of Mr Testo Sante, to the left beyond the stalls of the town cattle market, was burned down. The event we can see taking place appears to be some sort of trades procession, with all the horse-drawn decorated carts carrying advertisements on them. The street has changed very little since then. The old cattle market to the left is better known as the 'Flat Iron' today. To the right is the town bus station, which is to be removed from this site in the near future and relocated nearer to the railway station.

The Co-operative Movement in Chorley was established in 1887, succeeding previous short-lived ventures. The first shop of the new Co-op was in Lyons Lane, Chorley, and the first branch at Water Street, also in Chorley, in 1891.

In 1920 a block of shops was purchased at the corner of Fazackerley Street and Market Street, shown here. In 1922 a small shoe shop was set up, and the rest of the block rented out. Between 1930 and 1935, following attempts to sell the premises, it was decided to set up a clothing and shoe department, and the whole of the block was rebuilt. In the old photograph, the corner shop is about to be demolished, around 1933. The Co-op continued to use the building into the 1960s, when it was sold. Today, the building remains generally unchanged, and accommodates a travel agency and an estate agency. During 2000, all the property in Fazackerley Street beyond the former Co-op store was demolished, and the row is in the process of being redeveloped.

Market Street end of Fazackerley Street, looking along the street towards the covered market stalls. Beyond these are the buildings of New Market Street, which were demolished for the building of the new shopping mall during 1996. Among these buildings, and visible above the bus roof, was the public house called the Fazackerley Arms. To the left, the first building is the Co-op store, and next door is the Commercial pub. Beyond this appear several shops, and the new Queen's building, which became Boots chemist. The traffic more or less dates the photograph to the 1920s. In the modern view, some shops to the right have been rebuilt, while those to the left have been cleared prior to limited rebuilding. In the distance, the market stalls have been improved and beyond, in New Market Street, the new buildings of the shopping mall are visible.

Looking down Mealhouse Lane towards Market Street, the town hall is to the right of the photograph. In the centre distance is one of Chorley's former coaching inns, the Red Lion, which along with the Royal Oak and the Gillibrand Arms (where the town hall is now built), were all close together in the centre of the town. All of these hotels could accommodate stage-coach passengers and had stable accommodation for the coach horses. The buildings to the left were cleared in the later 1960s. The building immediately next to the Red Lion pub was the public hall, and it was in here that the very first films shown in Chorley were screened. The building later became the British Legion. On the extreme left is the entrance into Back Mount. Today the whole of this block is occupied by the pub formerly called the White Hart, which replaced the Red Lion. It is now possible to see Union Street in the distance, as the replacement pub does not project as far as the old one.

The main street through Chorley, formerly the A6 trunk road, now succeeded by a town centre by-pass, is shown here in the early 1950s, looking north, with the town hall in the centre distance. On the left is Messrs Foster and Co. motorcycle dealers. Next to this, and the tallest of the buildings, is the Royal, built in 1910/11 and opened in 1911 as the Theatre Royal. It later became a cinema, a role which for which it is probably best remembered. In its guise as a theatre, it had two balconies, which were retained in its cinema days, the upper balcony being known as the 'Monkey Rack', a place I have written at length about elsewhere. Suffice to say, as boys we were often ejected from this cinema for misbehaviour in that 'Monkey Rack'! When the Royal was demolished, the site hosted the first supermarket in the town, Whelan's. Several supermarkets later, the site is now occupied by a McDonald's burger restaurant. Just past the Royal, at the bottom of Gillibrand Street, was a pub, the site of which has been vacant for two years or so. Since the late 1990s, Market Street's footpaths have been widened, new street lamps have been erected as a Millennium project, and the road has been partially blocked to traffic, to create a pedestrian area.

This is Pall Mall, which then becomes Moor Road, which runs from Chorley towards Wigan. These two roads converge at the crossroads of Tootell Street and Weldbank Lane. The Mk II Ford Zodiac car is parked in Tootell Street. At each side of this street are old cottage properties, which were cleared during the late 1950s when it was finally decided that the crossroads should be made safer. There were no traffic lights here then, and the corner was almost a blind one, due to the old property blocking the view when emerging from Tootell Street. Emerging from Weldbank Lane was also hazardous, but not quite as bad as the street opposite. On the right-hand side, the Black Horse pub will be recognized, now with an open space alongside it.

Market Street once again, here viewed at its northern end, where it joins Park Road. The latter road was only built in 1822. Previously, the main road through the town had been via the road to the right of centre, Church Brow leading to Water Street, then continuing northwards. Visible in this 1960 photograph is, to the left, the building formerly called Terrace Mount, at one time a small row of terraced cottages. One of these was the home of the famous Tate family. Another occupant was one John Gray, who was town crier, bell ringer and parish clerk. The first post office in Chorley began in one of the houses at Terrace Mount. The building was refurbished in 1922 and began a new lease of life as the Trustee Savings Bank, a life that lasted almost to the end of the twentieth century, when the bank was relocated again. At the bottom of Church Brow are private houses, which later became a pub called The Swan With Two Necks. Above the trees one can see the roof of the former Parish Institute. Finally to the right, St Laurence's parish church.

Looking across what was usually referred to as the town hall square, when in fact it was actually called St Thomas's Square, we can see Mealhouse Lane in the distance. The photograph shows that demolition work has started, and the public hall has been demolished. As yet, the Red Lion still remains, along with its tap across the yard from the front house, which was the Red Lion itself. However, the pubs had gone by the end of 1961. The square in the foreground has been marked out to limit the number of cars using it. By 1964, the buildings to the rear of the square had all been cleared in advance of a new police station being built.

The town's main street had its origins several hundred years ago, the buildings there having been demolished and built over again. During these rebuilds, many of them have been moved back from the carriageway. On the other hand, some remained in their same position right up until the 1950s. One such group of buildings, between St George's Street and Chapel Street, was referred to as the 'bulge' during the 1950s. Perhaps the best known of this group of shops was a café called Christies. One of the great things about the café was that you could sit at the window seat and watch people passing by. It was certainly very popular. In the early sixties, as part of improvements to the traffic flow, the 'bulge' was removed by demolishing the row of buildings and re-building further back. Shops and offices are still on the Market Street site today.

When the Chorley town centre by-pass was built in the late 1990s, part of its south-westerly end incorporated the former Lyons Lane, shown here in 1958. In this view, we are looking along Lyons Lane towards its junction, around the corner, with Bolton Street. Starting at the left-hand side is a pub on the corner of Brooke Street, called the Victoria, then Brooke Street itself. At the top, in the left-hand corner, is the one remaining factory chimney in the town, saved despite its mill having been demolished. However, it is now a part of Morrison's supermarket complex, and certainly carries the highest advertisement in Chorley. To the right is a large stone-built cotton mill, which was one of Chorley's earliest steam-powered mills. The street from which the car is emerging is Standish Street, now no longer joined to the new by-pass road. All that remains today is the former Victoria Mill chimney.

This view along Lyons Lane, from 1962, was taken around the corner from the previous photograph, and looking in the other direction. The houses in the centre of the picture are the same as those in the previous photograph, as also is the end of Brooke Street in the centre distance. The building to the right is another pub, called the Green Man Still. This is the only building remaining at this location today, although it has now become offices. All the terraced houses are gone, and in their place the new town centre by-pass road. Just beyond the pub is a car park, which was used by management of the adjoining Victoria Mill when it was worked by Messrs Gainsborough-Cornard Knitwear. Prior to demolition, the mill was used by Pennine Cleaners Ltd.

Returning to Market Street again, c. 1960, at a time when it was customary for a policeman to be on point duty at the bottom of Chapel Street when the traffic was always heavy, especially at weekends. At this time, there was no M6 motorway to take all the north-south traffic; instead it all came through the centre of Chorley, as the main street was the A6. At weekends it was the coaches from the Midlands and the Manchester area that caused great queues through the town. During the week, it was heavy lorries on trunk work that filled the street. There weren't even any zebra crossings then. The white building in the photograph is Woolworths, either side of which was a bank. Woolworths has now moved to the shopping mall, and both banks have been rebuilt. This part of Market Street is now pedestrianized.

Chapter 2
People and Activities

Following the opening of Astley Park to the general public of Chorley in the 1920s, work continued on the former gardens and parkland, which had been private until then. Bowling greens and tennis courts had been provided, but little other than the open space, which forms today's playing fields, was provided for the younger element. Kite-making and flying was a popular pastime, and the open parkland was admirably suited to this activity. However, by the 1930s, a lake where toy boats could be sailed was being proposed. This came into being during the 1930s, much of the money having been raised from the work of the Chorley Round Table of the time. Today the paddling pool has been cleared away, yet it was donated to the town, and at this time is in need of replacement, along with up-to-date filtration equipment.

On the occasion of the commissioning of Chorley's new steam-driven pump fire-engine (although still of the horse-drawn type), this huge crowd of people attended in St Thomas's Square, at the back of the town hall during the 1890s. Following the speeches and the commissioning, the crowd and the pump were moved to the front of the town hall, where the boiler of the pump was lit and steam released to drive the new water pump. This was followed by a demonstration as to how high the water could be forced through the hose-pipes. Also visible in the picture is the corner of the town hall to the left, and to the right, the Rose and Crown pub, which is still there today. The former town hall square was greatly reduced in size in the mid-1960s with the re-building of the police station and new courthouse.

Another view of Astley Park, which was given to Chorley to form the town's war memorial by Mr R.A. Tatton of Cuerden Hall in 1919. It was to be the place where the town's cenotaph would be erected; this was subsequently built, along with other public amenities. The main gateway to the park, at the town entrance, was to be a focal point, and a suitable candidate for this was available at the entrance to another of Chorley's estates, that of Gillibrand Hall. The tall stone arch, decorated with flags and bunting, can be seen in its original position in Gillibrand Walks, along with the gatehouse into the parkland of the hall, to the left. The arch was decorated to celebrate the wedding of one of the Gillibrand family's daughters. Note the crossed swords of the Gillibrand family on the arch keystone. The arch was dismantled and removed to Astley Park entrance, where it was rebuilt with flanking gates.

One of the early commercial photographers in Chorley around the turn of the twentieth century was Luke Berry, who was followed by his son. Mr Berry was not just a studio photographer, but took his cameras out and about in the town, in order to record some of the events which have now been passed down to us, as part of our social history. One of Mr Luke Berry's photographs, taken at the end of the 1890s, shows a group of walkers from one of the town's churches, taking part in the town's annual Walk of Witness, here getting ready to set off on their walk through the town. The view was taken in Bolton Street close to its junction with Pall Mall. It is interesting to note the use of the flag of St George with a Union flag quartered on it. We see this particular flag on Royal Navy ships nowadays. The fashions may have changed over a century or so, but the procession and its purpose have not.

The first known postmistress in Chorley lived in the former cottages opposite the parish church, which were known as Terrace Mount, later the Trustee Savings Bank, where incoming and outgoing letters were taken to be processed from the nearby coaching inns. It was only during the mid-1850s that postboxes were first erected in London. These then spread around the country by the 1860s, but even then, they were found only in the larger cities and towns. The work of the Chorley post office increased after the railway came in the 1840s. This was a time when all mail had to be taken to and collected from the local office. It was only in the later nineteenth century that deliveries to households began. Contrast today's postmen's uniforms, which are suited to their particular area of work, with one of Chorley's early postmen wearing the uniform of the 1890s. Today's postmen have more than just a bag for letters – they often have a van for transporting parcels, like this Parcelforce worker.

If there is one thing which generations of Chorley children have always known about, it is the coming of Chorley Fair. After all, fairs and markets have been a part of Chorley's history for several hundred years, stretching right back to when they were granted by the lord of the manor in the King's name! In comparatively modern times, during the twentieth century that is, the coming of the travelling fair twice a year, meant setting up all the side shows and roundabouts on the market place called the Flat Iron, unfortunately clashing for the same venue with the traditional market. The roundabouts of the early 1900s, when the 'galloper' horses were a firm favourite, were driven by steam engines. In recent years, Chorley Fair has seen a move away from its traditional venue, to a railway goods yard, and to a street location along Market Street, here shown in 2000.

Another of the annual processions, similar to the Walks of Witness , in which the parishioners of the local churches walk through the town under their church banner, was the annual Chorley Carnival. Unfortunately, this venture, which raised much needed monies for local organizations, does not seem to have the same support now that it used to have. During the 1950s it was a different story, and crowds of people lined the routes to see the carnivals. In 1953, for example, Chorley Carnival was particularly special, forming the basis for the town's Coronation celebrations. Flags and decorations formed a dominant feature of the procession. The children in the 1953 Walking Day procession are pictured coming out of Lyons Lane and into Bolton Street, carrying Union flags. Almost fifty years on, the Jolly's fish and chip shop on the corner is gone, and the actual corner is much changed due to a roundabout having been built here.

In October 1953, the Duchess of Kent and Princess Alexandra came to Chorley to visit the Talbot Spinning and Weaving Company at Talbot Mill. The royal visit was made at the request of Mr Barber-Lomax, chairman of the board of directors of the company. During the visit, many local people were presented to the royal visitors. In its heyday, Talbot Mill was the largest mill in Lancashire, having a multi-storey spinning mill and adjoining single story weaving shed. The two sections were driven by separate steam engines. As the royal couple came to Chorley by car, their route was lined with spectators, shown here standing at the end of Pilling Lane and its junction with Bolton Road. In today's photograph, the spectators have been watching the town's annual Walking Day procession during June 2001, a time that sees Talbot Mill being demolished.

This is the Coronation Recreation Ground between Devonshire Road and Ashfield Road. Up to 1953, the only children's amenities had been swings, and what we termed the 'giant strides', which consisted of a tall iron post, around which dangled chains. At the bottom end of the chain, was a T-shaped handle. When we ran round the post holding the handle, we could lift our feet off the ground, hence performing 'giant strides'. It was a bit dangerous, I suppose, but it was good fun. In August 1953, a slide was built and was a great attraction. Today this part of the recreation ground is still a children's play area, now made much safer with wood chip on the ground. The house in the distance has been demolished due to coal mining subsidence. The second boy from the left is the late Roger Griffiths, brother of Peter, former primary school friends of mine. A modern slide has replaced the old one, and on it are, from left to right: Megan Marsden, Connor Claynose, and Connor Marsden, enjoying a slide forty years on from the original photograph.

Chorley Carnival is perhaps one of the most interesting street activities to look at. It also ensures that there are usually a number of people in the photograph as well! The year of this particular carnival was 1958, and the location is Devonshire Road at its junction with Regent Road. There are quite a number of interesting aspects about this photograph, besides the Carnival Queen sitting in the Singer Gazelle car (I wonder if that has survived until today!). Devonshire Road was one of the last of the town centre roads to receive tarmac. To the right, a few years later, would be Smith and Hodkinson's auction room. Today a doctor's surgery is built on the site.

This ceremony, attended by numerous clergy, is at a venue close to Bolton Road, during 1958. It was, in fact, a foundation stone-laying event at a new secondary school, then called St Alban's. The school was built on the site of an interesting old house, built in colonial style, and called Yarrow House. The foundation stone is still resting on wooden batons, and would be lifted and laid on its mortar bed after the service has finished. Today, it is not possible to take a photograph in the same location, for we would be inside the building. The present day photograph shows the wall with the foundation stone in it.

As we all know, crazes come and go. One that was all the rage in the early 1960s was the yo-yo, although this was not a craze appearing for the first time. Here a competition is in progress, thought to be at one of the Chorley cinemas, in February 1964. Remember how you could only make the thing go up and down, and everyone else could make it do all sorts of tricks? However, in 2001, the yo-yo is no longer at the top of the craze list, at least for the moment. The current craze is for small aluminium scooters, which appear to be competing with the skateboard for popularity. Pictured here is a trio of scooter enthusiasts, showing off their machines in 2001.

Chapter 3
Shops and Markets

Chorley Market, during the early 1900s. Chorley's first markets were held along the street, which was later to become Market Street. Markets were also held on the town green, close to the market obelisk. This later became St Thomas's Square, behind the town hall. The town stocks were also located here, so that the offenders would be seen by all persons coming to the market. In 1826, the market was relocated to its present site by Mr H.H. Fazackerley, lord of the manor, who had the street approaching the market named after him. Fish stones were set up, and the stocks and water pump were relocated here, although the stocks were burned in a fire in 1855.

The notices which appear in the window of a Chorley newsagent's shop give us the clues we need to estimate when the picture actually dates from. The notice on the left of the doorway tells of a 'Mafeking special' in the *Lancashire Evening Post*. The notice to the right tells us about the British advancing and about what the Boers were up to. All these activities refer us to the period of the Boer War, which took place from 1899 to 1902. The shop of Mr John Threlfall was a varied business, as can be seen by the shop sign, operating as printer, bookbinder, newsagent, tobacconist and tea dealer. Similarly, Mr Brian Straw's modern newsagent's shop in Pall Mall, Chorley, also displays boards relating to news headlines, in addition to showing its other activities, such as being a National Lottery station.

In this old view of a Chorley shop front, we are looking at the grocer's shop of Messrs T. Harling and Company, which was located towards the Gillibrand Street end of Avondale Road, adjoining the ginnel which ran through to Westminster Road. The shop delivered goods to its customers in the Pall Mall to St Thomas's Road area using the horse-drawn delivery cart shown in the photograph. The premises are still used as a shop today. Now it is known as the Two Worlds Christian Book Centre, which has been established in Chorley for some twenty-five years, recently celebrating this anniversary with an 'open house' on 7 July 2001.

The north of Chorley: Preston Road and the A6. Just off to the left is the entrance to the Crescent estate, while off camera to the right, was a wall behind which was a large fishpond and Chorley Hall Farm. Looking across the road, there is a long row of small cottages, which have been vacated prior to demolition. The one exception is the shop, visible in the centre of the photograph, which sold flowers and vegetables. Note also the two 'up steps' houses next to the garage and to the left of the car. These were handloom weavers' cottages at one time. All this old property was cleared at the end of the 1960s. The whole of the block behind the cottages accommodated North Street Cotton Mills, or Smethursts, as it was more commonly known. Today the area is occupied by large retail outlets such as B & Q and Comet, as well as the ambulance station and other smaller outlets.

The gentleman's outfitters of Messrs Clarkson, located in Cleveland Street, was one of those so-called 'old established family businesses', having been passed down from father to son. The shop at this time was next door to a pub called the Clarence, which survived into the late 1950s. This pub adjoined the alleyway that is Back Fazackerley Street. In June 2001, the old shop site is occupied by a shop called Box Clever. The old shop occupied the right hand side of the modern shop only. The modern shop doorway is in the same place as the doorway to the left in the old picture; there is a side entry to the left, still visible.

Market stalls and shops on Market Place, probably photographed from upstairs in the pub that used to stand at this site, the Fazackerley Arms, during the 1950s. The view looks over the market stalls with shops to the left, such as Dennis Hoban Fireplaces; Meadows self-service grocery store (supermarkets had not yet arrived); Adam Barnes' bookshop; the Victoria Arcade; and Sharples on the corner. Above the arcade was the Arcade Café, which was extremely busy during market days. Across Cleveland Street, beyond Sharples, the side of the Clarence pub is visible. The Maypole shop and Smith Fielden's fish and poultry shop can also be seen.

This view from around forty years ago was photographed in Steeley Lane, at the east side of the railway through Chorley, which has often been said to have cut the town in two. At this time, there were many shops in the street. In the centre, where the white Ford Corsair car is turning, is Little Steeley Lane, on the corner of which was the Regent Cycle Store, where many of us got our first cycles from in those days. Continuing up the lane, one came into Seymour Street, and thence to Eaves Lane. It was a busy shopping area during the 1960s, but has become less popular today. Some of the shops have now been demolished, some are propped up, and all the buildings that were in Little Steeley Lane have been knocked down to be replaced by modern council property. It is no longer possible to drive into Seymour Street from Steeley Lane.

The market, viewed from the upstairs window of Messrs Brimley and Co, leatherware manufacturers, located at the corner of Fellery Street with Union Street. Based on the cars, it is probable that the photograph was taken around the mid-1950s. The Refreshment Bar, removed when the new shopping mall was built, can be seen here. Incidentally, this first appeared soon after the Royal Ordnance factory began production in 1940, and it provided welcome drinks for workers awaiting buses. In the background on the left lie the buildings in Clifford Street, and to the right, the sawmill works of Messrs Haydock and Company. Fifty years on, trees have replaced factory chimneys, but the Flat Iron market, despite fears that it might be lost to the town, is still alive and well today.

The Victoria building in Cleveland Street, with its popular arcade. The building was erected in 1893, and was certainly very much a part of the Victorian period, which is now largely lost to Chorley. The building was certainly functional, having Messrs Darlington and Sons barber's shop in the basement, all the shops at ground level; also the arcade itself was always a good place to shelter from inclement weather! The first floor was occupied by offices and a café. However, readers may recall the dance hall on the top floor (the Vic, we called it), run by Albert Entwistle. This was a place that was very popular with the young people of the time, and where ballroom dancing was taught to all ages of aspiring dancers. Today's building looks almost clinical in comparison with the Victorian architecture. It certainly does not possess the character of the old building, which is perhaps something being eroded from the townscape of Chorley as a whole.

Unfortunately, there is neither time nor space to tell all of the old stories regarding the Market Place area, but one building which particularly merits mention is one that first started life as Chorley's first co-operative shopping scheme. This failed towards the end of the 1890s, but subsequently the building went on to accommodate Chorley post office and Chorley technical school. The building was purchased by the Chorley Co-operative Society, a new venture in 1887, and opened as a draper's, dressmaker's, milliners, tailors and outfitters in 1906. It was one of those shops which was a memorable place to visit as a child: it had a lift to the upper floors - these were few and far between in Chorley shops - and the staff wore uniform clothing. Speaking of memorable shops, I suppose we must mention Booths, with its smell of ground coffee. The Co-op was still using the building into the 1960s. Since then, the shop has had many occupants, and is currently a Poundshrinker shop.

Chapter 4
Private Houses

One of the town's older streets is Hollinshead Street, named after a local benefactor who had a town house at the top of the hill in the photograph. The street runs between Water Street, where it joined Church Brow, and Clifford Street, at its junction with Bengal Street, both now incorporated in the town centre by-pass road. Walking eastwards along Hollinshead Street from what used to be Church Brow, now Church Steps, you climb a steep hill. From the bottom of this hill to the junction with Clifford Street, was a continuous row of mixed types of terraced housing, which lasted until the early 1950s. All these are now gone, except for three garden-fronted houses.

Of the two chimneys to the right, the taller was the destructor chimney, demolished in 1950. The smaller chimney was at Mayfield Mill. Both chimneys were situated off Stump Lane.

Preston Street, once a part of the main road through the town in the days of the stage-coach, is now part of the town centre by-pass road, giving access onto Preston Road, the route of the former A6 trunk road. Our late nineteenth-century photograph shows how it used to be, with old terraced property to the right. The backs of these houses overlooked a triangular yard called Mill Court, with access via the short street in the middle of the photograph. All the properties were built by local mill owners for their employees. This site was cleared in the 1930s and remained largely unused, other than being a scrapyard annexe. A temporary ambulance station was built here in the 1950s. In the 1990s, the site was taken over by B and Q home improvement store.

The centre of Chorley, around the town hall and the parish church, is the oldest part of the town. Despite numerous rebuildings of old properties there, parts of the old town remained into the 1950s. For example, there were three 'one up, one down' cottages in Back Mount, standing next to the former Red Lion tap, pictured here in 1948. The three houses shared one yard and one lavatory, and could be accessed through the gate at the far end. I knew the occupants and visited on occasions. Despite their 'one up, one down' configuration, they were clean and tidy (note the 'donkey stoned' steps) but obviously ready for demolition. Following their demolition in the early 1960s, a new pub, the White Hart, was built to replace the Red Lion. The rear of the new pub is on the same building line as the old cottages were.

As stated elsewhere, many of Chorley's older stone-built properties were originally handloom weavers' homes, with loom-shops in the cellars. These houses dated from early to mid-nineteenth century, and were located in small communities in and around the town. The largest of these communities was to the east side of Bolton Road, incorporating King Street and Queen Street. By the mid-1950s, this area of the town was rather rundown, and the houses were generally in a poor state of repair, but most of them were still occupied. Many of the living room/kitchen areas did not have sinks, but the old stone 'slopstones'; none had hot water or bathrooms; and some groups of houses shared a common back yard with outside toilets. By 1959, some of the occupants had been moved out, prior to the demolition of the houses. Today this area has been built over with council property, but the mill chimney remains.

Former handloom weavers' cottages, Bolton Street. If one looks under the large window to the extreme left of the old photograph, it is possible to see some large stones forming lintels for the cellar window, now blocked up. These windows would of course allow light into the cellar loom-shop. Many of these houses which were on Bolton Road and Bolton Street had been converted into shops, but all were originally weavers' cottages. All the cottages were demolished during the mid-1960s. Today garden-fronted council property faces onto Bolton Road.

During the mid-1960s, the route of the proposed new M6l motorway was made known, which would affect people living in the Botany area of Chorley. The new motorway would pass to the east side of Chorley, cutting through the outskirts of the town at its north-east sector at Botany Brow. Here the motorway would cross the canal 300 yards to the left of the old photograph, then cross the road in the immediate foreground of our picture, necessitating the clearing of the houses to the left and right. About 200 yards to the rear of the houses on the right, was the former Chorley to Blackburn railway line on top of an embankment, with a viaduct over the canal. These also had to be removed to make way for the new motorway. The new bridge over the canal and motorway made the modern view rather difficult to obtain.

Park Road was also a part of the main A6 trunk road through Chorley, running northwards towards Preston. To the east side of that road, and running parallel to it, is Parker Street, which runs between Park Street, at the far end of our picture, and Commercial Road, which is 'behind' the camera. This street too has seen much demolition of old property, including houses and the pub on the corner, but at the far end of the street, on the left, a group of handloom weavers' cottages have been preserved, refurbished, and are still occupied. Hidden by the trees in the centre distance, is Park Street Unitarian chapel, whose benefactor was Mr Abraham Crompton, the purchaser of the former Chorley family estates in 1718. The railings just visible to the far left surround what used to be the playground for the Parish Church Boys School. Today this is a pre-school, and the modern day view down this same street shows some of the school frontage.

I expect many Chorley residents will not know that we used to have a second Pall Mall in the town, but the proof can be seen in this mid-1950s photograph. This was one place in the town, which I recall as being almost Dickensian in its layout. The street was actually called Back Pall Mall, the name and entrance to it being alongside the gable end of the Eagle and Child pub. Upon entering this short dead end street, around you were the backs of old houses, many of which had been handloom weavers' cottages in the past. Some idea of the size of this court-type street can be formed from the photograph. Today shops replace the old houses to the left and centre, with a car park and garden area next to the Eagle and Child pub.

Pall Mall in Chorley runs west from the town towards Coppull and the A49 to Wigan. Close by the crossroads of Pall Mall and Moor Road with Tootall Street and Weldbank Lane, is a pub called the Black Horse. There was a short street alongside the pub, which is to the left in the photograph. This was probably the narrowest street in the town, and was only just a little wider than a car. The street was cobbled until the time of its demolition in the 1960s, when large areas of the town were declared unfit for habitation. The name of the street was Black Horse Street. The houses in the distance in the old photograph front onto Tootall Street. Our modern photograph shows where the street used to run, in between the Black Horse pub and the adjacent council property.

Here is another late 1950s photograph, showing some of the older houses around the town. These were in an area lying a little off the beaten track, in that it was some distance from the centre of the town. This row of old cottages, which had gardens to the front and back, was in a short street called Little Cart Lane. The cottages were, before the new houses were built on Carr Lane itself, part of a small community with a street called Red Bank, which had been built close to the Duxbury colliery. The cottages were built for the men and their families who worked at the pit. The community had its own chapel of worship called Red Bank chapel, a building which remains in use today. In the modern photograph, new houses stand on the site of the old cottages.

Looking down Cowling Road, back towards Chorley town in the distance. To the left is the building which was Hall o' th' Wood mill, which had a wharf on the canal alongside, where bales of cotton brought from Liverpool were unloaded. The road bridge over the canal can be seen above the two white cars in the photograph. As mentioned previously, some old domestic properties in Chorley were built for people working in mills and collieries by their employers, and this was indeed the case here with these one and two storey stone cottages. All the property shown in the photograph was demolished during the 1960s and early '70s. A chemical works and a brewery distribution centre have now been built behind where the houses used to stand.

Lyons Lane in Chorley, during the 1960s. This stone-built property used to stand just past the end of Little Steeley Lane, visible to the left of the photograph. Also just visible at this corner is the white building which became the Co-op emporium, and at the end of the row of stone buildings, the very first Co-operative shop in Chorley which was established in 1887. This was located at No. 81 Lyons Lane and was rented for seven shillings a week. Due to the presence of cellar windows, it is probable that these old houses were used for cotton processing and, quite possibly, spinning as the cellars were not very large. Following their demolition, council property has been built at the same location.

Chapter 5
Views around Town

The front of the Queen's hotel in Chapel Street at the corner with Victoria Street, *c.* 1890. The hotel had stables and a coach-house, and the coaches were largely for the use of patrons of the hotel. The hotel was/is only a short distance from the railway station, which must have been to its advantage, while across the street from the hotel was a smithy. The Queen's, as the hotel is known today, is still a popular town centre venue.

Market Street, *c.* 1890. At that time, it is apparent that some of the properties had thatched roofs. Whether or not they were shops is uncertain, but the likelihood is that they were. This street was the first to be established in the town, and the first houses were built along that early road. It was here that markets, including livestock sales, took place, and at various points in history, many armies have passed along the street. It is of interest to see that Messrs Brindle and Sons, Furniture Sales, were delivering their goods by horse and cart. Generally speaking, the layout of the street is the same today, but many properties have been rebuilt.

The railway system of the Lancashire and Yorkshire Railway during the early years of the twentieth century meant that their trains ran to Chorley, then continued north west, to the North Union Railway line at Euxton junction on the Wigan to Preston Railway. Some six miles or so north of Chorley is town called Bamber Bridge, and this line also belonged to the Lancashire and Yorkshire Railway. In order to gain more passengers, the railway introduced a bus service in 1907 between Chorley and Bamber Bridge stations, passing through all the small villages on the way. Our old photograph shows the railway bus at Whittle le Woods during one of its runs. There is no longer such a service between railway stations, but the old route has become part of the normal Chorley to Preston bus service.

It is unusual to be able to date the older photographs exactly, but this one definitely originates from January 1934. It shows work being done to widen the canal bridge at Botany. The parapet wall of the bridge to the right of the car has been removed, and steel girders are being fitted to carry the widened roadway. This area changed greatly with the coming of the M61 motorway, which is 'behind' the camera position. We are looking across the canal bridge towards Blackburn Road, with Knowley Brow off to the right. A new canal bridge was built in the late 1960s, to the right of the photograph, to span the canal and the motorway. Yet the old canal bridge at Botany Bay, often referred to as the port for Chorley, is still in place, side by side with the new bridge. Also of interest are two old pubs, the Railway to the left and the Roebuck to the right. The Railway is the only survivor today.

Chorley's third grammar/technical school was built in Union Street, and was opened in 1906 by the Earl of Derby. It succeeded the Queen's Road school that had opened in 1868, which itself replaced the first grammar school, built in Church Croft, alongside the parish church. During the 1920s, Chorley saw the introduction of its first bus service, although there was no bus station. The buses started from St Thomas's Square; the Flat Iron market; and Union Street, in front of the school. This building became too small to house the school and a new school was built in Southport Road in 1962. The Union Street building was subsequently adapted to become a teacher training college.

Today, part of the building accommodates Chorley Central Library, opposite which is Chorley's bus station.

One of the most surprising aspects of the main street in Chorley, is that it used to be so very narrow in front of the town hall: in fact, it was only half the width it is today. However, between 1936 and 1937, the old property was cleared in order to widen the road and to build behind the old buildings. In this view from High Street, across from the old entrance into the post office, the new building that was to become the Odeon cinema nears completion, and alongside the Odeon, a new building is taking shape. This was to become a new Royal Oak pub. At this point, the old Royal Oak was still in the process of being demolished, and its roof timbers can be seen, with the town hall clock tower behind. Many changes have taken place here in recent years, with shops now occupying the area where the pile of rubble can be seen in the old photograph.

Reference to the post office in the previous photograph prompted me to select this late 1940s view, which shows the west side of the post office (where the present entrance now is), viewed from the rear of the Royal Oak hotel, looking across the hotel car park. This area has since been built on, and this vantage-point is no longer available. The post office has been much enlarged, to the extent of having another storey built. The present-day view is from the right, at the bottom of High Street. The photograph probably dates from August 1946; and the large queue of people stretching from the bus station to the left, and around the corner into High Street, are thought to have been visitors to the Royal Lancashire Agricultural Show in Astley Park, now awaiting transport home.

The unusual sight of elephants walking out of Market Street into Fazackerley Street! They were with a visiting circus to Chorley and had come by railway to the goods yard, where they had been off-loaded, watched by a large number of children. They were walked via Market Street as part of the circus procession that took place to advertise its arrival. In the background, Woolworths can be seen at its old site in the main street, whereas today it is lost in a shopping mall. At either side of Woolworths were banks; these were the District Bank to the right, and Williams Deacons to the left. Both are still banks and have been rebuilt, sadly with the loss of the architectural features the previous banks enjoyed.

Union Street, December 1956. There are several points of interest in this view. Firstly, there is the narrow width of Union Street, which was later widened. On the left is the Imperial hotel, at a time when it was a popular venue instead of being the semi-derelict building it is today. Next to the pub was the Ribble bus office, and beyond was Hughlock and Hindle's garage: the queue we can see was for petrol. The site of the garage is now occupied by a Chorley Borough Council civic building. In the distance are houses in Clifford Street, later demolished to make way for the town centre by-pass road.

The old view is taken from an original post card by Valentines, and would appear to date from the 1890s, if we consider the clothes being worn. We are, of course, looking up Chapel Street with the Shepherds Hall building in the distance. On the right is Jardine's grocer's shop with Blackburn's hat shop to the left. In the centre, at roof level, is painted 'Luke Berry and Son, Photographers', whose photographs reveal what the town was like at that time. The busy scene gives us an insight as to how little the street and its shoppers have changed over the past century or so. Our modern photograph was taken after Walking Day 2001, when the walk's spectators were moving away up Chapel Street to do their shopping.

Another annual Chorley procession is a civic one, taking place soon after the appointment of a new mayor, usually in April. The procession accompanies the new mayor to his or her particular church. Also taking part are town councillors and various local organizations. The procession starts at the town hall and proceeds via the main street to the church. In our old photograph, we see the Mayor's Sunday procession of July 1954, as it approaches the end of Market Street, and turns around the big lamp at the end of Pall Mall. Of particular interest are the shops in the background, from the left: Odell's cycle shop; Baker's gun shop; Booth's café (a favourite place to call at after going to the pictures); Bibby's shoe shop, at the end of Cheapside; and finally Owen's Travel, next to the electricity showroom. Today many of the shops have been demolished, and a new extension was built for Runshaw College next to the old electricity showroom during 2000.

Further down Market Street, at the bottom of St George's Street, a new pedestrian crossing was created in 1958. This was after complaints from people who found it was virtually impossible to cross the road, especially at weekends, such was the volume of traffic passing through the town en route to Southport, Blackpool and the Lake District. At times, solid queues of traffic stretched all the way from the town hall traffic lights to Bolton Street/Road. Following the installation of the crossing, it was monitored for a while to see how effective it was. Today the crossing is still in the same position, but it is now pedestrian-operated, and on a street which sees less traffic due to the town centre by-pass road.

With all the new traffic flow schemes introduced around the town centre during the 1950s and into the 1960s, it was not surprising that many of the proposed routes were difficult to work, due to hold-ups affecting schedules. At one time, traffic going north came out of Fazackerley Street, and traffic going south came out of Chapel Street. Along with other the improvements, including widening, Union Street was made one way only (for traffic coming into it from Market Street) for a trial period. During this time, trials were conducted with double-decker buses, to ensure they could enter Union Street safely when coming in from the south. Here one such trial is underway in wet conditions. Note the old Red Lion pub at the end of Mealhouse Lane to the left.

The bottom of Church Brow, looking back up the Brow to the parish church gates to the left of centre, with the town hall tower just visible through the trees to the right, August 1964. Work is underway to block the old road by filling it with shale brought in to build up the embankment which would support the widened Park Road. This job was done to allow better traffic flow along the main A6 trunk road, as Park Road was then. Perhaps now that we have yet another A6 road, we could one day see the old Church Brow opened up again, as less traffic uses Park Road now. Since these works to block off Church Brow, in the mid-1960s, the building to the left has become a pub called the Swan with Two Necks. Our modern photograph shows how the new embankment looks today, which perhaps could benefit from some terraced planting and seating close to the top of the steps by the parish church.

The end of Clifford Street and its junction with Chapel Street, early 1960s. To the right is the Shepherd's Hall building, while the shop on the corner is a photographer's called Photo Movie. However, the reason I include the photograph in this section is due to the number of times that traffic was held up just around the corner, as wagons were being loaded and unloaded at the main doors of Messrs Haydock and Company Limited, Timber Sawmills and Merchant. If the hold-ups were not here, they often occurred a little further along Clifford Street, where large curing and stacking sheds for the timber were the scene of wagons backing in and out. Later, when the sawmill closed down, the building became Morrison's supermarket. Our modern view shows the building has gone, to be replaced by the delivery yard associated with Woolworths and Boots in the new shopping precinct.

Many alterations took place at West Street around 1970. Up until this time, West Street had been an 'unadopted' street, which was so rough you took a risk with your car springs if you drove down it. The works undertaken saw the street built up, close to the rear entrance gates to the former Rawcliffe Hospital, Chorley's first hospital. This raised portion became the present car park accessed from Devonshire Road. The photograph shows this work in progress. To the left is the old St Mary's Hall, and many will recall the dances and concerts held there. To the right is the closed Rope Works, which was being altered to accommodate other business ventures. This later became the Weldbank Plastic Company. Today, after rebuilding, St Mary's Hall has become St Mary's Parish Centre. The rest of the area is a car park.

Chapter 6
Railway and Canal

Today, seeing a photograph of a steam locomotive evokes memories of the past; after all, their use came to an end back in 1968. Yet, for some inexplicable reason, they are still a major attraction at all the steam preservation centres, or when 'steam-hauled' specials are run. Yet when they were around in the fifties and sixties, they were generally looked upon as just another part of the scenery; no-one other than the spotters and enthusiasts revered them. Chorley is located on the Manchester to Blackpool line, between Bolton and Preston. In this photograph, which dates from February 1958, a steam train en route to Bolton is stuck in snow at Grimeford Cutting, Adlington, one of Chorley's villages.

Looking along Railway Street to the warehouse, March 1963. The railway arrived in Chorley on the route of the Bolton to Preston Railway, building from the direction of Bolton. Due to problems north of Chorley, where a tunnel was being bored, a temporary station was built in Railway Street in 1841, where a goods yard was later to be created. Following completion of the tunnel in 1843, the station was re-sited in its present main line location. The goods yard began to be used as intended, and a large warehouse was built. The whole of the goods yard was cleared away in the mid-1990s to make way for the new town centre by-pass road. Our more recent picture shows the embankment for the new road, and a truncated Railway Street.

Between 1841 and 1843, it was realized by the townsfolk that when the line was completed, they would only be able to cross the railway line to get to the shopping area of the town by walking to the intended rail bridges at Lyons Lane and Stump Lane. This was because when the subway at the intended new station built, it was to be used by rail passengers only, and not as a public thoroughfare. As the railway had cut the town in half, so to speak, people ran the gauntlet of crossing the tracks until, close to the new railway station, a bridge was built. However, many ignored the bridge and still crossed the lines, and as a result several were killed. Subsequently, the bridge was replaced by a public subway, which emerges close to a new bypass road.

Passengers waiting for a Blackpool train at Chorley station, June 1959. Our Chorley railway station has, since its opening in 1843, seen some rather special events, but no royal visits, despite many royal trains having passed through the station. It was built on the Bolton to Preston Railway, which became a part of the Lancashire and Yorkshire Railway system, and this connected with all parts of Lancashire and into Yorkshire, and allowed Chorley folk to travel more extensively than they had done previously. The busiest times at Chorley Station until the mid-1960s were in June and July. This was a time when cotton mills closed for their annual 'Wakes' holidays, and trains to coastal resorts were always full. The modern photograph shows how the same platform has changed, with its canopy and bay platform for Blackburn/Wigan trains removed.

Although Chorley became incorporated into the Lancashire and Yorkshire Railway network, a rival company, the London and North Western Railway, built a line between Wigan and Blackburn in 1869, passing through Chorley station. From Chorley, the line climbed towards Blackburn, and often necessitated the use of a banking engine to push the train from the back. The Blackburn line bridged Harper's Lane, on which was painted the advert CEPHOS, the name of a well-known medication, and this lent itself to the name of the bridge. In our old photograph, dating from about 1961, the sign has been removed, and the railway is still in use. Our modern photograph shows that the bridge has gone, along with the embankments either side. Houses are now built to the right, where the embankment used to be.

The Botany viaduct, viewed from the canal bridge at Botany Bay, c. 1950s. After passing over the bridge in the previous photograph, then along a half-mile embankment, the Blackburn line crossed the Botany viaduct of nine arches, of which only eight are visible here. Beyond the arches lies the cotton mill of Messrs Widdows and Company, called Canal Mill, which now accommodates the complex of Botany Bay villages. With the disclosure in the mid-1960s that the proposed M61 motorway was to pass through this area, it was realized that this great architectural feature would have to be demolished, for trains were no longer using the line. The edge of the new motorway passes through where the second arch from the left was.

During the late 1960s, the new M61 cut a swathe through the Chorley countryside from Anderton to Bagganley, crossing the canal to Botany. After considerable preparations, including the insertion of explosives into each of the columns, the ninety-nine-year-old viaduct was ready for demolition. This took place early on a Sunday morning, on a dull and drizzly November day in 1968, and a number of people assembled, ready to see the end of this great stone feature. After several delays and false alarms, there was a series of muffled explosions, as shown in the photograph, and the viaduct was no more. The present day photograph, although not quite at the same position, shows what changes have taken place, with some of the old landmarks still visible, such as the mill complex of Botany Bay villages.

The Chorley district is well served by train services, despite having lost some of those services when the Wigan to Blackburn line was closed, the villages of Adlington, Croston, Hoghton, and Euxton all having their own railway stations. In Euxton, a village that has had four railway stations, has recently had one replaced. This is at Balshaw Lane, where the original railway station on the Preston to Wigan Line, was demolished in the 1960s. Our old photograph shows the old station at the end of its life, the access steps down to the platforms being closed. With the rebuilding of the station at Euxton's Balshaw Lane, came many objections due to the lengths of the access ramps, and the fact that houses had, since the 1960s, now been built on the Chorley side (to the right), of the fast line tracks. The long ramps overlooked the houses and were brightly lit, as can be seen in the more recently taken photograph.

Botany Bay in Chorley had both railway and canal associations. It was firstly a canal centre, and after the building of the Lancaster Canal in the late 1790s, became the port for Chorley. It also became a community in its own right, some two miles from the centre of Chorley town. The older properties hereabouts were mostly built from stone, as with these old cottages on Knowley Brow. The old photograph shows the railway viaduct still in place, before 1968. The canal is just visible in the centre, just above the street lamps. Today the cottages remain the same, some forty or so years on, and the M61 is now visible in place of the old railway viaduct.

The coming of the new motorway through Botany, not only led to the loss of the ninety-nine year-old nine-arch railway viaduct, but also the loss of an old canal warehouse. The warehouse was alongside the canal basin at Botany, hence the name Botany Bay being applied to the basin itself. The warehouse, which dated from the early nineteenth century, is shown to the right hand side in this old photograph, which dates from the early 1950s. The road bridge at Botany is shown, and just visible is the railway viaduct. As the M61 motorway was routed to the left of the photograph in 1968, a wider span bridge was needed to cross the canal and the motorway. This was built over the old warehouse, which was demolished along with the property to the left. The present day photograph shows how different this view is today.

Moving south from Botany, a series of two wide sweeping bends in the canal look in the direction of Talbot Mill, which was also known as Bagganley. Between these two bends, the M61 motorway crosses the canal via a skew bridge, continuing south beyond the overhead power lines to the left of centre. The mill in the distance was one of the largest in Lancashire: the four-storey part of the building was for spinning, with a single-storey weaving shed at the far end. Raw cotton and coal was brought to the mill along the canal. The mill had two steam engines to drive the machinery, one for the spinning rooms and one for the weaving shed. In the late 1990s, the four-storey mill was demolished, and this was followed in 2001 by the closure and current demolition of the weaving shed. The 1960s photograph shows the mill with its tower, but today so many trees are growing here, it is only possible to see the canal itself.

This original coloured postcard was postmarked 22 December 1905. It shows a view of the canal looking back towards Botany Bay from the canal bridge adjacent to where the mill would be built a little later. It also depicts open vistas with, above the canal boat, the roof of the chapel at the top of Knowley Brow, and a wide well cared for towpath to the left. Now looking back towards the bends in the canal and Botany Bay, nothing but trees can be seen on the canal bank, and even the M61 bridge is hidden.

British Waterways men are preparing the bankside foundations for a new metal bridge to replace the wooden one, in May 1957. This particular part of Chorley is one that will be recalled by many of the children of the late 1940s and '50s, for this was a popular spot at which to swim. The old wooden footbridge across the canal was on a path from Eaves Lane to Crosse Hall fields and the 'rush pit'. Another interesting point about the old photograph is that it shows the adjoining field undisturbed and not yet built upon. The building in the distance is, of course, the former Chorley Union Workhouse, which by the 1950s was part of the complex called Eaves Lane Hospital. Note the unusual shape of the chimney to the right. A new chimney was built when the whole boiler house was later renewed. Today, even this fine Victorian-fronted building has been cleared away, and houses have been built all the way down to the canal at each side of the footpath from Eaves Lane.

A very popular type of trip during the early 1950s was that of the canal boat outing. This sort of trip was particularly favoured by organizations such as Scouts, Boys' Brigade and church groups, such as Sunday schools, plus local clubs etc. The canal boat outings were popular because they were cheap and provided something different. One of the favourite places to visit was Haigh, where the end of trip picnic was held. In our old photograph, dating from the 1950s, the wide barge has a full cargo of passengers on such a day outing, which usually started from Botany Bay or Froom Street wharf. The photograph was taken from the Crosse Hall Lane bridge. Nowadays, numerous pleasure boats use the canal and are moored at Top Lock, as seen in the modern photograph.

Chapter 7

Buildings Altered or Demolished

The parish church of St Laurence had, at one time, a large parcel of land, in addition to the graveyard, to the south side, which extended across the present day Union Street. This was referred to as Church Croft. It was in this croft that Chorley's first grammar school was built, between 1823 and 1824. Another building located here was a barn, which has been termed a 'tithe barn'. This has reputedly been removed to Botany Brow, where it survives today as a garage. The original school was succeeded by a new grammar school in Queen's Road during 1868, the former becoming a savings bank until 1933 when it was demolished. In the old photograph, a date-stone can be seen above the gable window. This stone survives today, and can be found in the parish church wall in Union Street, on the site of the old grammar school.

Looking from Park Road down to the row of houses into Water Street that replaced earlier cottages, c. 1968. At the bottom of Church Brow, the river Chor used to be visible, through which the coaches passed via a ford. From here, the river flowed into the then private land that was Astley Park. It was here also that the main entrance to the park of Astley was located, prior to Park Road being built in 1822, when the gatehouse was relocated to the new road entrance. Beyond the houses in Water Street is the Bowling Green, which was at the rear of the Parish Institute, which fronted onto Park Road. To the top right we can see the old parish rectory. Our present day photograph shows that the institute and the houses have been demolished, to be replaced by the modern Georgian-style 1990s tax office for the Chorley district.

The oldest building in Chorley is the parish church of St Laurence, which has its recorded origins in the fourteenth century, although an earlier church may have once have stood on the site. The old families of the town, such as the Chorleys, the Gillibrands, the Standishes, and the Charnocks, all worshipped here, and are buried within the church. The church is linked with Myles Standish, who sailed to the new colonies with the Pilgrim Fathers. The church only became independent from the mother church in Croston in 1793. During 1860, the church with its nave and tower was enlarged by the building of the two aisles. During 1998 and 1999, new parish rooms were built at the south east end of the church. These can be seen in the modern picture.

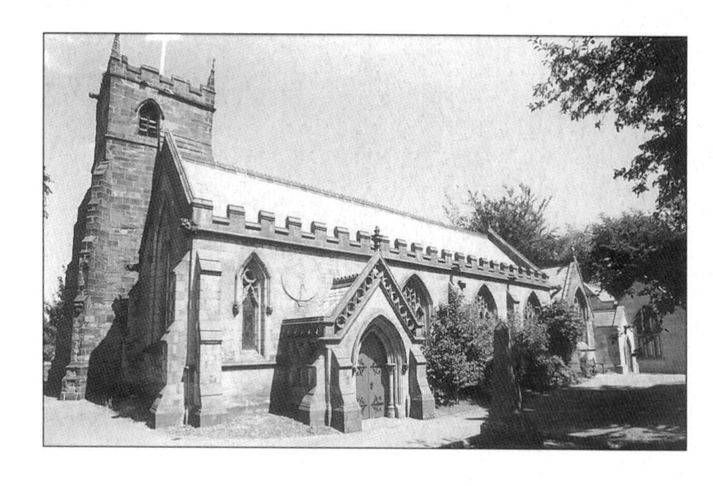

I don't suppose there are many towns that have had two town hall buildings, even for a short time, but we did in Chorley. The first town hall built in Chorley, in 1802, was provided by John Hollinshead, of Hollinshead House, Chorley, and it stood in a street named after the family. This new town hall was erected on the corner of Market Street with Union Street. The stone building had offices and rooms on the upper floor, which were used by the town's board of guardians, the predecessor of the town council. The ground floor of the building was used as a farmers' market where fresh produce was sold. In 1879 a new town hall replaced the old, and in 1881 the town received its Charter of Incorporation to become a borough. The old town hall was demolished in the mid-1930s. The modern photograph shows the town hall as it is today, now in its 122nd year.

If you had walked down the side of the old town hall into Union Street from Market Street during the early 1930s, this is the view that you would have seen, looking east along Union Street to its junction with Clifford Street in the distance. Remember that, at this time, the street was not immediately adjoining the parish church graveyard wall as it is today, but was almost in line with Mealhouse Lane. There was also a steep hill, with old property either side of the roadway. On the left can be seen an alleyway. This led into a court in Church Croft, where the old grammar school, later a savings bank, used to be. The present day photograph looks along Union Street as it is today. To the right of the modern photograph is Chorley bus station. This is to be relocated near to the railway station in 2002.

When the streets and roads of Chorley were being named, it was popular to give names that were being used in London, for example, we have Pall Mall and Fleet Street. It is the latter which is the subject of our photographs on this page. The older photograph here dates from the mid-1960s. The older houses in the street, which were to the right-hand side, were demolished at this time. On the left, at the corner of Cheapside, the corner house used to be a public house. Behind these properties, was a communal yard with shared outside toilets. At the end of the street, across Pall Mall, is part of St George's School extension and the Church Institute. Our modern picture shows that the old houses and Church Institute have now been demolished; the institute has been replaced by a large store.

It is indeed unfortunate when architecturally interesting buildings are demolished, particularly when a town does not have an excess of such buildings. It seems a waste that another role has not been found for them. One such building in Chorley was the former library, located in Avondale Road. It was built due to the generosity of Mr Parke of Withnell Fold, and was opened in 1899 with a Mr McKnight as its librarian. By the 1990s, the old building had become too small for the library's needs, and the library was relocated elsewhere. The old building was stripped and demolished: among the things that were dumped was a brass plaque commemorating the first librarian. This was found by the author in a Manchester scrap-yard, and brought back to Chorley where it was presented to the library during its centenary year, 1999. A health centre now occupies the former old library site.

Another of the town's buildings with its origins during the Victorian era was the former Chorley workhouse, pictured here during the early 1950s. Following closure of other local workhouses at Brindle and Croston, the Chorley building became Chorley Union Workhouse. During the late nineteenth century, a much larger building was constructed to the west of the original workhouse and fronted onto Eaves Lane. By this time, the workhouse system was moving towards hospital status. By the 1960s, the building complex had become part of the Chorley and District Hospital. During 1998, this grand building, one of Chorley's finest period buildings, was demolished, to be replaced by yet more houses. Today, the outer wall and the railings that fronted the hospital are all that remain of the original complex of buildings.

One of Chorley's less grand buildings was situated in Water Street, and is shown here in July 1956, having been much enlarged since the 1830s. This was the Chorley gasworks. The large building to the right was the Retort House, where coal was burned to remove its volatile material and gases and turn it into coke, a process which produced much dust and smoke. To the left are great piles of coke (which were good to slide down on tin sledges) awaiting sale. In the late 1940s it was possible to go and purchase sacks of coke at the works, which you filled yourself. The works were gradually cleared during the 1960s and '70s. Today houses are built on the site, their low garden walls created from the wall by the footpath seen in the old photograph.

Looking down St Thomas's Road from the end of Dole Lane, at the old police station, during the late 1950s. Between the station and Crown Street was the house of the Police Superintendent. Chorley saw a new police station built between 1964 and 1965, which created quite a controversy due to its architectural style being out of place when compared with the nearby Victorian town hall. Many suggested it should have been built across Southport Road from Parklands School, to create a matching pair of modern buildings that would be seen when approaching Chorley from the west. Adjoining this new building was a new courthouse, and both the police station and court house were entered from St Thomas's Square. These new buildings replaced an earlier police station with integral courtroom. In the modern photograph, the new building entrance via a bridge over a large fishpond can be seen.

This old photograph dates from around 1960, and shows the building which dominated this site until the 1990s. This was where Market Street, Pall Mall and Bolton Street met, and where, from the 1860s, a big cast-iron lamp post stood. This lamp, with its three sets of gas mantles, was nicknamed the 'big lamp', and was a popular meeting place. The lamp was removed in the early 1950s, instead of being converted to electricity. The building in the photograph began life as the National School in 1825, becoming St George's Primary School in its later years. The 1960s photograph shows the school with church institute in Pall Mall before demolition. The site is now occupied by a modern stores building, which has had at least two occupants in the short time that it has been built. A replacement 'big lamp' was erected in the mid-1990s.

Chorley Co-operative Society property, located in the middle of the street, at the junction with West Street, *c.* 1963. The buildings of Market Street in Chorley, are still generally on the same line as they were in the eighteenth century, despite many of them having been rebuilt. Indeed, the rebuilding is still incomplete: in some places, demolition has taken place, but rebuilding on the site has not yet happened, even after two years or so. Along the length of the street, many of the oldest buildings still have random stone-built walls, although the fronts have been re-built in brick. In the late 1960s all of this block up as far as Bleasdale's was cleared, and the whole of it rebuilt, as shown in our last modern photograph.